2006 PRESIDENTIAL ADDRESS

ADS ON TIX
(A Review of Commercial Advertising on UK Transport Tickets)

given by

Hugh Fisher

To a meeting of the Society at
The Southwick Community Centre,
Southwick, West Sussex
on 17th February 2007
and subsequently repeated at
The Friends Meeting House,
Mount Street,
Manchester
on 10th March 2007

SPECIAL NOTE REGARDING ILLUSTRATIONS

In order to accommodate the number of illustrations in this publication, it has been necessary to reduce the dimensions of certain tickets. This has not, however, affected any of the pre-grouping or pre-nationalisation edmondson card tickets which are represented as true facsimile. The same applies to road motor and tramway punch tickets, Insert Setright, Setright Speed and Ultimate tickets. The tickets concerned are identified by an asterisk against the relevant illustrations plus an additional comment denoting actual size.

The remainder are reduced by 20% with the majority of the Wayfarer tickets "cropped" but still retaining the relevant features noted in the text.

The Transport Ticket Society
2010

This publication is sponsored by Ticketmedia, the leading authority on UK ticket advertising and a speciality manufacturer and printer of ticket rolls, primarily for the transport industry.

For full product information and contact details visit www.ticketmedia.com.

The production of this publication has also been made possible thanks to the bequest to the Society by the late Courtney Haydon who was a member for about 34 years

Further copies of this and other publications may be obtained from the Society's Publication Sales Officer:

Steve Skeavington
6 Breckbank
Forest Town
Mansfield
NG19 0PZ

Comments etc. regarding this publication are welcome; please write to the Hon. Secretary,

Alan Peachey
4 The Sycamores
Bishops Stortford
CM23 5JR

Published by

The Transport Ticket Society
4 The Sycamores
Bishops Stortford
CM23 5JR

© Hugh Fisher 2010

ISBN 978-0-903209-65-6

Printed by

DOPPLER PRESS
5 Wates Way
Brentwood
Essex CM15 9TB

INTRODUCTION

Gentlemen. I am honoured to have been your President over the past year, particularly as the Society celebrated its Diamond Jubilee in 2006. The Jubilee weekend and dinner held in the Netherlands during October was a very convivial occasion and I must express our thanks to our Dutch members who laid it on so well. I have also attended several of the Society's Executive Committee meetings during my time in office and gained an insight into the efforts that go on behind the scenes to keep the show on the road. This is not always a painless process and there have been some fairly frank exchanges between certain of the Society's key officers. Changes in the membership of the committee are taking place (new faces are Alan Peachey, Steve Skeavington and Nigel Tarrant) and it is my hope that all those involved will be able to work together constructively for the benefit of the wider membership in the years ahead. In particular our Chairman, John Tolson, is standing down at this year's AGM after six years in office, and I would like to thank him for the energy and commitment that he has brought to the task - largely unsung and not always appreciated - and wish him well for the future. Indeed, I would thank everyone who has served or is serving on the committee for the work they do and the time they put in to making things happen for the rest of us.

Enough of the plaudits, let's get down to the subject in hand. In this presidential address I hope to carry out a fairly quick review of UK transport tickets carrying commercial advertising material. That is, advertising other than the operator's own publicity material. It will have to be quick because the scope of the topic is enormous, covering pretty well all modes of transport from the earliest days of tickets up to the present day.

In the 1998 membership survey, the results of which I don't think were ever comprehensively published, the "Advertising on Bus Ticket Rolls" section of Journal was ranked lowest in terms of interest - just 18% of respondents found it "always interesting", while 44% stated it was "never interesting". So I guess that means delivering an address on the subject is going to be more of a challenge, if you are not going to glaze over or nod off. I would mention that I did only take over editorship of the column in 1998 (the same year as the survey) and have tried to make it topical as well as providing a running record of all known advertising rolls as they have appeared. But fear not, I don't intend to bog you down with boring "bogofs" (buy one get one free offers) or an endless litany of advertising panels. I would rather share with you what I have found interesting - even attractive - about modern-day adrolls, and that is primarily the influence that the advertisement has had on the design of the ticket front. Over the past fourteen years this has been evident more than any other period in the history of transport tickets, with the exception, perhaps, of very early omnibus tickets. These resembled the front page of Times newspapers of the same era, carrying more advertising than journey-related data.

However, let's step back for a few moments and look at advertising in a broad context. Whether we like it or not, whether we think that the presence of commercial advertising enhances or spoils the appearance of a ticket, the fact is that the promotion of goods and services is a long-established practice and is here to stay. Anyone who has something to sell or offer will seek to gain custom through advertising, using a wide variety of media. These will include the familiar, such as billboards, posters, newspapers, magazines, radio and TV, along with the modern-day phenomena of the Internet, telephone "cold calling", leaflet drops and even such improbable outlets as urinals and petrol pump nozzles. Anything, in any place where your attention might be gained for just a few seconds. So it is not surprising that transport tickets have succumbed to this treatment. The Ticketmedia website speaks of tickets as being "the poster in your pocket" and claims that during a typical bus journey, people with nothing better to do will avidly study a bus ticket advert and then (potentially) go straight out and buy whatever is on offer. There are many advertising agencies seeking to win custom by promulgating all manner of goods and services, and most organisations - with the possible exception of the TTS - have a budget for advertising, to be spent in whatever way proves effective. It is big business, with some firms spending millions of pounds advertising their wares.

I am certainly not an advertising professional, so my observations and remarks are very much of a lay nature. There may well be people here who have a greater involvement in the advertising industry and who are able to add further insights into the way the whole thing works. We are primarily looking at the medium itself - the actual tickets - rather than the mechanisms to produce them or any of the commercial influences, design work, printing processes, analyses or reviews that take place, however important these are in the whole advertising cycle.

I would actually like to concentrate on the latter-day phenomenon of advertising on modern bus tickets - which is, of course, the section I look after in Journal. I am more familiar with this era than with earlier types of advertising and my own interests have focussed particularly on collecting Wayfarer tickets over the past thirteen years. However I have, perhaps somewhat incautiously, cast the net rather wide in using the term "transport tickets" in the title of the address. So I am honour bound to include advertising on rail tickets, and that is where we will start, back in the pre-grouping era (pre-1923).

Pre-grouping Edmondson card tickets

This is not an era that I have pursued in my own collecting interests, so I am grateful to Michael Stewart and Brian Pask for assistance they have given.

Surprisingly few pre-grouping railway companies used the backs of their tickets for commercial advertising, and those that did were often among the smallest operators.

The mighty **Great Western Railway (1)** is only known to have carried two commercial adverts. An arrangement with Imperial Union Assurance commenced in 1871 - this was a railway-related service, but provided by a third party, so qualifies for inclusion. Then in 1908 an advert for Lipton's appeared. It was a very basic form of advertising and took for granted that everybody knew that Lipton's was a brand of tea. However this means of advertising was hastily discontinued after unexpected objections were received. One wonders what the substance of these objections might have been!

(1)

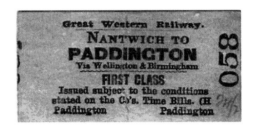 

By contrast, the **Great Central Railway (2)** was far more prolific, with numerous adverts known from merchants, outfitters and suppliers of all manner of goods and services, based within their operating territory. So we have companies like Boots of Nottingham, Claytons Teas of Mexborough, Crow of Chesterfield, Stewart & Stewart of Sheffield, Speed's of High Wycombe, Chapman Bros of Banbury and the Queen's Hotel, Southport. Others are known from companies based in Ashton (under Lyne), Barnsley, Brigg, Cleethorpes, Doncaster, Gainsboro', Grimsby, Loughborough, Leicester, Lutterworth, Retford, Rugby, Rotherham, Scunthorpe, Wembley and Worksop - and probably elsewhere. The GC clearly had an eye to the commercial potential of their tickets. Print quality, however, was variable.

(2)

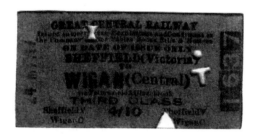

Another major company that took advertising seriously was the **Metropolitan Railway**. We can look in a little more detail at the Met, with the benefit of Brian Pask's researches. Hardly any Metropolitan tickets carried conditions on the back and one can speculate whether this was a deliberate policy intended to foster commercial exploitation. Adverts had appeared as early as 1869 **(3)** and the company actively sought custom through their advertising agent, Willing & Co. In this early period (only), certain tickets with the station names in large initial letters carried the legend "See Back" to draw attention to the advertisement **(4)**. The layout of a non-advert ticket front is also shown for comparison. From 1873 there seems to have been a dearth of adverts, but in 1892 a series of five "Cherry Blossom" toiletry (not shoe polish) adverts appeared **(5)**. Notice the use of engraved illustrations - quite a step forward in technology for advertising on tickets. Where the front of the ticket bore a red "O" or "I" overprint, this did not appear on the back if an advertisement was present. Another lull followed, since we are not concerned today with the railway company's adverts for their own services, and it was not until 1910 that a sole advert for Whiteley's of Bayswater appeared. There was a final burst in 1915/6, with State Express Cigarettes and Wrights Coal Tar Soap appearing in a series of four mildly humorous line drawings **(6)** - all of very good quality. And that was it, with no further adverts on the Met before its absorption into the LPTB in 1933. [cf: Ticket History Volume 1 No. 2 - July 1991]

(3)

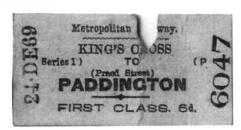

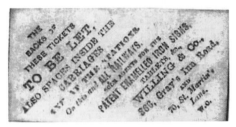

(4)

(5)

(6)

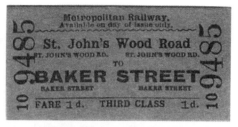

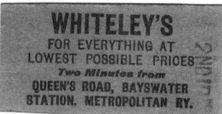

From the heart of London to the bustling quaysides of Liverpool. **The Liverpool Overhead Railway Co.** (7) sported a handful of advertisements, notably for Kydd & Kydd's Jams. Examples seen date from the 1901-1914 period.

(7)

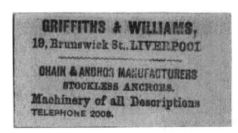

Likewise the **Mersey Railway (8)** had a few advertisements around the same period, plus one for Beecham's pills a little earlier. Old Calabar promoted bulldog meal, game meal and chicken meal on various tickets. Beecham's were a prolific advertiser, particularly on early London tram services.

(8)

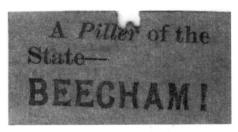

Two very small but contemporary concerns in East Anglia were the **Lynn & Fakenham Railway (9)** and the **Yarmouth & North Norfolk Railway (10),** which had combined in 1882 to form the Eastern & Midlands Railway. A couple of adverts are known from each concern, plus one for "coal and coke at Yarmouth prices" (although this may have been a railway company advert). These adverts appeared on tickets of both the YNNR and the **Great Yarmouth & Stalham (Light) Railway (10)**. Pre-grouping tickets don't come much rarer than that!

(9)

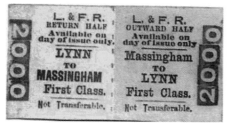
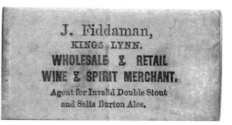

(10)

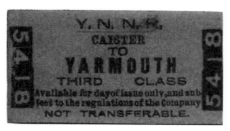

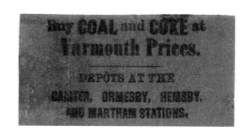

The **Isle of Wight Railway (11)** had a couple of advertisements, in the 1880's.

(11)

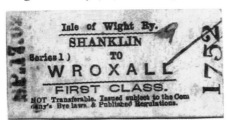

All early tickets of the **Isle of Man Railway** and the **Manx Northern Railway (12)** carried an advert for "Greensill's Mona Bouquet", obviously a major contract.

(12)

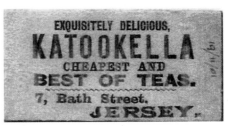

To round off the pre-grouping edmondsons, we head for the Channel Isles, where there was a profusion of advertisements on the three Jersey railways. Here is a selection from the **Jersey Railways & Tramways (13),** dating from the late 1890's to the early 1900's.

(13)

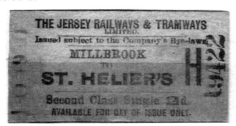
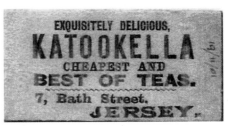

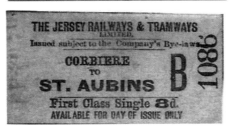

The **Jersey Railways Company (14)** included the legend "This space to be Let for Advertisements" on the back of some of their tickets. This even appeared when an advert was already present, so maybe the contract had expired and a subtle pressure was being applied for its renewal!

(14)

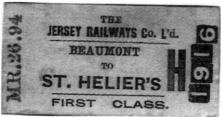

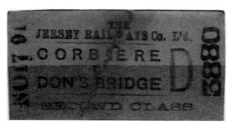

Finally the **Jersey Eastern Railway (15)** carried adverts at least until 1929, with numerous examples noted from Noel & Porter Ltd, in several different formats. A minor aside, but each Jersey railway company seems to have had its own clientele of advertisers, with little overlap between them.

(15)

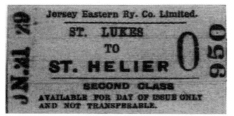

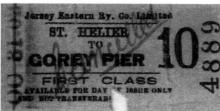

Other pre-grouping railway tickets

We will just take a passing glance at some non-edmondson tickets with advertisements, from a few concerns.

In the capital, the **Waterloo & City Railway (16)** had a few adverts like this on pre-grouping punch tickets, but the backs were mainly used for L&SWR in-house advertising.

(16)

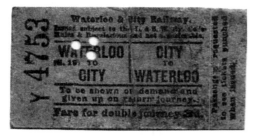 

The **Cleobury Mortimer & Ditton Priors Light Railway (17)** carried adverts for the local ironmongers and drapers on some if its punch tickets. These would date between 1908 and 1922, when the line passed to the GWR.

(17)

Further south, the **Hundred of Manhood and Selsey Tramways (18)** carried an advert on their roll tickets for Adolphus Ballard, in his several manifestations, and his successor in title TE Jay.

(18)

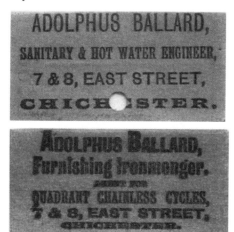
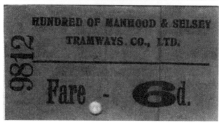

Finally the **Rye & Camber Tramways (19)** attracted a selection of local advertisers to their roll tickets, printed by both Williamson and an anonymous supplier.

(19)

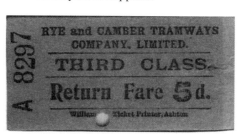
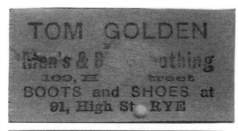

Pre-nationalisation edmondson card tickets

By 1923, the backs of railway tickets were usually blank or printed with conditions of issue. However, the London Midland & Scottish Railway went in for a bit of innovation by producing a number of edmondson tickets with a "pull out" advert interleaved in the pasteboard. These date from the early 1930s. Here is one actually issued in 1964 **(20)**, with its pull-out advert for Pratts Motor Oil **(21)**. Various types of ticket appeared in this format, including platform tickets. Michael Stewart classifies these platform tickets as LMS type 2B: Ashbourne and Chalk Farm **(22)**. Bromsgrove and Bromley **(23)** are ex-Midland section hybrids of LMS type 2BH. These four tickets were all issued in 1932. Examples of "pull out" advert platform tickets have been noted from 31 stations in all.

No other pre-nationalisation railway company is known to have had commercial advertising on the backs of its edmondson tickets and the same applied throughout the British Railways era.

(20)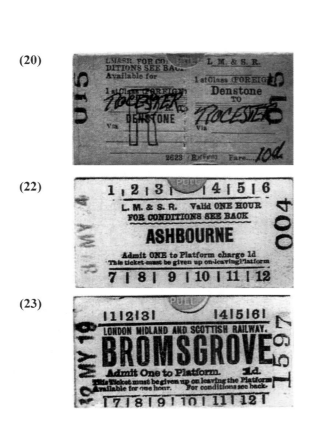

(21)

(22)

(23)

Road motor and tramway punch tickets

Now we move into a more familiar and prolific field. Advertising on the back of road punch tickets was widespread in both London and the provinces from the late 19th century onwards. The late Jack Purton, in his 1972 presidential address, dealt with the vast range of advertising on punch tickets, particularly in the pre-1914 era, when the scene was dominated by adverts for drapery stores and patent medicines.

We have time only to note a few examples in passing, from a more recent period **(24*)**.

- Bolton Corporation (Charnley's)
- Crosville Motor Services (handkerchiefs - who would have paid for that one?)
  Halifax Corporation (Quick Shoe Repair Service - with Bell Punch block no. A2094)
- Pontypridd Council Transport (TV Ale - from Ely, near Cardiff)
- Ipswich Corporation Trams (Flangola, complete with riddle: Q - Why is a rosebud like a promissory note? A - It matures by falling due.)

(24*)

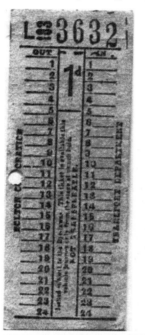

* actual size

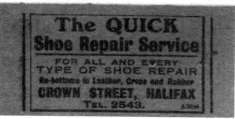

Adverts from agents seeking business appeared from time to time - examples are known from Pioneer Omnibus, London (Henry Squire) and Burton-upon-Trent Corporation (Courtenay). There were doubtless others.

We have already noted that there were a few examples of railway punch tickets that carried adverts.

Advertising on punch-type tickets returned in the mid-1990s, with the horse bus services to Covent Garden and the London Zoo. These used replica punch tickets printed by Keith Edmondson, as reported in August 1994 *Journal (*page 292), some with an advert for Kodak on the back.

Bellgraphic

The only examples I have found are from the Isle of Man Road Services (Jacobs Cream Crackers) and Jeffs Coaches (CF Brown & Sons) **(25)**. The Isle of Man advert was also featured by Paul Smith in his 1999 Presidential Address on Bellgraphic tickets.

(25)

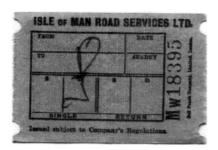

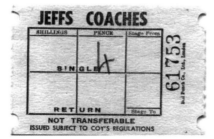

Setright Speed

There are plenty of examples from a variety of operators. Featured here **(26*)** and **(27*)** are a few examples from up and down the country.

- Brighton Hove & District (French Railways Motorail Services)
- Merthyr Tydfil Corporation (Robart hairdressers)
- Middlesbrough Corporation (Dents soft drinks):

(26*)

* actual size

- Plymouth City Transport (Olivers footwear)
- SELNEC PTE (Barchester British sherry)
- Thames Valley Traction (Belmont Labs - pregnancy testing)

There were also advertisements on some Setright rolls in the mid-1990s, of which more anon.

(27*)

Insert Setright

Not quite so common, but here are two **(28*)** from:

- Aldershot & District Traction Co. (Float Iron Laundry - Bell Punch block no. A1345)
- Hants & Dorset Motor Services (König lager - BP block no. A8081)

(28*)

* actual size

TIM

I didn't think there were too many of these until Paul Smith kindly sent me a bundle of TIM tickets with adverts! The following 33 operators are known to have had advertising rolls:

Accrington Corporation
Belfast Corporation
Blackburn Corporation
Blackpool Transport
Burton Corporation
Bury Corporation
Colchester Corporation
Darlington Corporation
Darwen Corporation
Edinburgh Corporation
Great Yarmouth Corporation
Grimsby & Cleethorpes Transport
Haslingden Corporation
Leigh Corporation
Liverpool Corporation
Lowestoft Corporation
Morecambe & Heysham Corporation

Northampton Corporation
PMT
City of Portsmouth (CPPTD)
Provincial
Rawtenstall Corporation
Reading Corporation
Rochdale Corporation
St Helens Corporation
South Wales Transport
Southdown MS
Stockport Corporation
Swindon Corporation (and Thamesdown Transport)
West Hartlepool Corporation
Widnes Corporation
Wigan Corporation
Yeomans Motors

They date from the period 1951 (Southdown MS) to 1984 (Thamesdown Transport). I have excluded CIE from the list as being outside the UK. Here's a selection (29) from:

- Morecombe & Heysham Corporation (Bare dry-cleaners)
- City of Portsmouth (CPPTD) (Snookies delicatessen) - issued to myself on the Hayling - Eastney ferry in August 1959 [when I was a mere lad of 14]
- Reading CT (Howell's cycles)
- Swindon CT (Hobby's Corner)

(29)

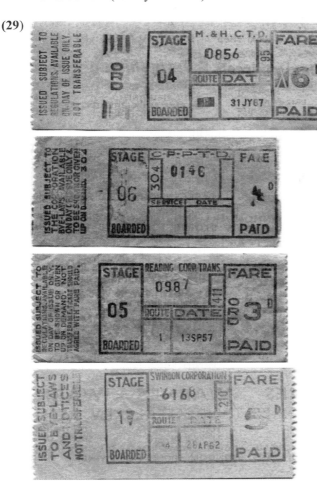

Ultimate

Usually the backs of these tickets were blank or read "Go by Bus", but a number of adverts exist, like these examples **(30*)** from:

- Bournemouth Corporation (Brewer Cowl - BP block no. A7280 ?)
- Huddersfield (City de Luxe shoes)
- Kingston-Upon-Hull CT (Humber Ports Annual - BP block no. A4004)
- West Bromwich Transport (Dartmouth Garage and The Plaza)

(30*)

* actual size

Gibson

The only adverts I am aware of are those produced for London Transport in 1977, in conjunction with the Queen's Silver Jubilee and used on the twenty five silver Routemaster buses. There was a short article on the subject in the March 2006 *Journal* (page 97). Here we can note an example **(31)** from SRM23 aka RM1902, featuring Tate & Lyle's Mr Cube and the misquotation from the book of Judges - part of Samson's riddle to his in-laws "Out of the eater came something to eat, out of the strong came something sweet" [not the other way round].

(31)

Almex A

Blackpool Transport featured several adverts on their Almex ticket rolls like this one **(32)** with a discount offer for K Shoes (Dec 1993). Note inclusion of the operator's title on the back - a practice that would become quite widespread. The Crime Stoppers advert was on the back of a Lincolnshire Road Car Company roll. The ticket is dated 1992 but the same roll was in use with Redroute Buses of Northfleet on London Buses route 185 in 2002. There were also advertisements on some Almex A rolls later in the 1990s, of which more anon.

(32)

Timtronic & Almex Magnet

We now move into the era of first generation electronic ticket issuing equipment. Only a very few examples are known before the mid-1990's, any printed matter on the back usually comprising the operator's own publicity. However a 1989 PMT Timtronic (part of a series of adverts) and 1991 City of Gloucester Magnet (Ludlow Financial Services) can be illustrated **(33)**. On the back of the PMT ticket you can just read through "Don't just sit there! Advertise here".

(33)

Farestram & Autofare

This was another piece of first generation electronic ticket issuing equipment, again with only a sprinkling of commercial adverts **(34)**.

- Busways (Elswick [I think] Park & Pool) - part of a series of adverts

(34)

- Preston Borough Transport (Wilmington). Preston did feature quite a variety of advertisements, so were obviously more commercially minded.

There were further advertisements on Farestram and Autoslot rolls in the mid-1990s, of which more anon.

Early Wayfarer Mk 2

No adverts are known on Wayfarer Mk 1 tickets, which were in any case small and dismal! There was some use of commercial advertising in the early days of Wayfarer 2s, as exemplified by the following **(35)**:

- Reading Buses (Four Horseshoes, L Eighteen and Simply Floors) - 1992
- South Yorkshire Transport (AFG, Doncaster) - 1990
- Merseybus (Prescot Shopping Centre) - 1991

Many more, of course, were to follow.

(35)

Note that on all these early examples, the printing technique is quite basic - generally monochrome and with fairly limited artistic design. Information was conveyed in a functional manner and the products advertised were, by and large, basic household requisites and other goods and services aimed pretty much at the adult market.

The Advertising Revolution on Bus Tickets

All the old order was about to change! It was into the scenario of monochrome, basic artwork designs that a small firm called the Britannia Roll Manufacturing Company Ltd, of Hove, began to market advertising on the back of bus tickets in the autumn of 1992. Up to that time the staple product of this firm, as its name suggests, was till rolls. They adopted the trading name of Image Colour Roll Promotions, subsequently shortened to Image Promotions, and changed in summer 2000 to Ticketmedia. This firm has been the leading, if not quite the sole, player in the field of bus and rail ticket advertising virtually since their inception. In August 2006 ownership changed to Canarycliff Ltd, following a short period of administration.

Britannia recognised the potential of bus tickets as a medium to reach a younger target market - those who by reason of age or limited means made use of public transport rather than private car. Accordingly the products marketed were those with an appeal to this age group, and so we saw the beginnings of what turned into a tidal wave of advertising for fast-food products. Not only that, the adverts themselves exploited the use of colour and pioneered much more ambitious design, using computer-based technology for both design and printing. Furthermore, Wayfarer 2 and 3 tickets offered more scope for improved design since a much larger area of space was available than, for example, on a Setright or Almex A ticket. Nonetheless, the multi-colour technology was not limited to Wayfarers, as adverts were produced in due course for most of the heritage systems then in use with the larger bus companies.

This is a convenient point to begin our consideration of modern ticket roll advertising, both road and - to a lesser extent - rail. Britannia's first known foray into the field is believed to have been two 1992 promotions for McDonald's, one with Bluebird of Middleton, the other with Ribble Buses (Chorley). Here they are (36), typically offering some deal on presentation of the ticket. The fronts of the tickets follow the general design then in use by the two companies but in their detail are unique to these promotions. They also show that Britannia had not yet mastered the technique of spooling the rolls the correct way round in relation the machine-printed data! (It is not the result of the driver loading the roll upside-down in the machine, which would cause the journey data to appear on the back.) The Ribble ticket is from a Mk 2 machine, Bluebird from Mk 3 although not programmed to include any stage names. Little must Paul Smith, the then Road News editor of *Journal*, have realised what was about to come when these two rolls were - very fully - reported in the March 1993 *Journal* (page 111)!

(36)

(37)

Blackpool Transport also used Wayfarer 2s, initially on the trams, and their tickets carried a Burger King promotion in 1992 (37), but this was not a product of Britannia (it may have come from Keith Edmondson, who also printed tickets rolls, including some commercial advertising). In early 1993 a McDonald's promotion for Accrington, Blackburn & Burnley appeared on Hyndburn Transport's Timtronics, again not a Britannia product, as reported in May 1993 *Journal* (page 198) (38). Merseybus also had a McDonald's promotion with validity to the end of January 1992, from their regular roll supplier, and North Western Road Car sported a McDonald's offer for Skelmersdale on their Almex Magnets, both reported in June 1993 *Journal* (page 242).

(38)

The next known Britannia promotion was with Mainline (Wayfarer 2) for another McDonald's offer, valid at any restaurant in South Yorkshire or Chesterfield, as reported in July 1993 *Journal* (page 298). This ticket included the imprint "Image Colour Rolls" for the first time, along with their 0273 telephone number **(39)**.

(39)

Concurrently Keith Edmondson produced a Burger King roll, also for Mainline, and this is of particular interest in that the Burger King logo appears on the face of the ticket, with the slogan "See over for promotional offer" **(40)**. This practice would soon be taken up by Britannia, as we shall see. Around this time, Keith also produced a Microfare roll for London Pride, valid at various McDonalds outlets in London, as reported in September 1993 *Journal* (page 346), but with a blank front.

(40)

By mid-1993 Britannia had obviously decided this was a winning formula and the bus ticket advertising industry moved up a gear. This is evidenced by a snippet recorded in August 1993 *Journal* (page 334), indicating the existence of other new advertising rolls from Trent, Barton and Sussex Bus **(41)**.

(41)

But it was not until November of that year that Roger Atkinson, who had by now taken over from Paul Smith as Provincial Road editor, recorded 15 new rolls from Britannia, as well as several more from Keith Edmondson. The range of products advertised began to grow as well, including disposable nappies, tenpin bowling and photographic processing. The vast majority, however, were for fast food products, mostly from Burger King, Kentucky Fried Chicken, McDonald's and Pizza Hut. Ticketmedia now quotes 1993 as its effective start-up date, so the very first rolls were doubtless of a trial nature. There may, of course, have been others - we only know what has been reported in Journal! At this point I must record my gratitude to Roger Atkinson for the very thorough reporting in the early days of what turned out to be a vast number of promotional rolls. He adopted the columnar format in Journal that is still used today, albeit with some modification. As can so often be the case, this was a period of rapid change and development - in the field of advertising rolls as well as in the bus industry as a whole - and if a comprehensive record had not been made at the time, much of this information would be very difficult, if not impossible, to retrieve.

Britannia introduced two features that deserve mention. The first was the inclusion of the advertiser's logo and a slogan on the face of some bus companies' tickets - as pioneered by Keith Edmondson earlier in 1993. It is interesting to note that some operators appear to have taken a deliberate decision that they did not want this feature on the front of their tickets; Stagecoach Hampshire Bus was one such and there are many others whose tickets never carried an advertiser's logo on the front (eg: Cardiff Bus, Eastern Counties, London Transport Buses). There are a good many early examples of tickets <u>with</u> the advertiser's logo, from companies such as Inverness Traction, Luton & District, TMS & Tees, Trent Buses & Barton, United, United Counties and Yorkshire Rider. Note that they are all relatively major operators.

Incidentally, Ticketmedia always refers to what we call the front of the ticket as the "back" - to them the front is the advert side.

At this time the advertiser's logo was generally printed in its own distinctive colours, irrespective of the colours used for the rest of the front of the ticket. These colours were:

- Burger King - red and orange **(42)**

(42)

- Kentucky Fried Chicken - red (red and blue on Ribble and United Counties) **(43)**

(43)

- McDonald's - red or red and yellow (red and yellow with a black slogan on West Midlands Travel) **(44)**

(44)

- Pizza Hut - red and black **(45)**

(45)

- Jolly Roger (Peterhead) - red and black **(46)**

(46)

However, it clearly didn't take the printers long to realise that producing multiple colour fronts added unnecessary cost to the process, so from around August 1994, the advertiser's logo, where it appeared, was printed in the same colour as the rest of the ticket. There were a few exceptions to this rule and the date the change took place varied from one bus company to another, but in no case was it later than the end of 1994.

Nearly all the tickets with the advertiser's logo on the front were Wayfarer 2 or 3 rolls. However there is one example known of a Farestram ticket, from Southampton Citybus, complete with a KFC logo on the front, as reported in February 1994 *Journal* (page 41) and two Almex Magnet tickets, both from Go Ahead Gateshead, with a Burger King logo. Of these, one is red and orange, the other all-red. **(47)**

It is also worth noting that these tickets always included a slogan on the front, like "Make the best of…" or "Have a treat on …". The slogan would generally refer to the bus company, rather than the product on the back!

(47)

As the range and quantity of advertising tickets increased over the next few years, so more advertising logos and slogans appeared (by now all on Wayfarer 2/3 ticket rolls). These have appeared from time to time in the occasional *Journal* colour feature "A Feast of Advertising Logos". A list of all known logos and the bus operators with which they appeared is set out at the appendix. There are thirty eight different company logos known, many for firms that advertised only once or twice - like the Jolly Roger. In addition, there were two styles of the Burger King logo, two of the Kentucky Fried Chicken logo and five different representations of the Littlewoods logo. That makes forty four varieties in all.

Let's have a look at some of the other logos that have appeared from 1993 onwards:

- five Littlewoods styles **(48)**
  L1a Littlewoods RESTAURANTS (plural) - no flourishes (TMS & Tees)
  L1b ditto - with flourishes (Bradford Traveller, First Bradford & Southport only)
  L1c ditto - interlinked letters, no flourishes (Clydeside 2000 - unique)
  L2 Littlewoods Restaurant (singular) (GM Buses North, Greater Manchester and East Yorkshire only)
  L3 Littlewoods (Stagecoach East Midland)

(48)

- Pepsi Max (as part of one national KFC+Pepsi Max promotion in early 1995) **(49)**; this logo only appeared on the blue-printed tickets of 5 operators: KHCT, Stagecoach East Midland, Stagecoach Ribble, Stagecoach United Counties and Yellow Buses, Bournemouth. Other rolls in this promotion carried the KFC logo.

(49)

Here are some more unusual advertisers (50 and 51).

- Homestyle (Trent Buses)
- Discotheque Royale (GM Buses North)
- Reliance (Reading Buses)
- Elgringo's (Yellow Buses)
- Power Drome (KCB Network)
- Richeys Fitness Club (Strathclyde's Buses)
- Stevenage Festival (Luton & District)
- Tennessee Fried Chicken (SWT)

This is, of course, only a selection. But how many others were there of which we know nothing?

It was this particular feature - the advertiser's logo on the face of the ticket - that first aroused my interest in modern advertising on tickets. In early 1994 there was a vast, nationwide promotion for Kentucky Fried Chicken featuring an identical advert panel with numerous bus companies. One of these was Reading Buses, whose otherwise brown-printed Wayfarer 2 tickets included a bright red KFC logo (43). Subsequently many others came to light and the reporting of these tickets in Journal, under Roger's expert hand, was most commendable (Roger classified them as "note 2 - multi-coloured advert by Image Colour Rolls on back, but also with advertiser's logo on front"). It soon became clear that if I were to locate and obtain examples of each different variety from every bus operator that had them, I would have to pay close attention to the listings in Journal, to the extent that I was often able to add information and reports of my own. Let me state here and now that it was not the advertisements themselves or the products or services they were promoting that drew my interest; I am certainly not eulogising fast food, legal aid, shopping centres, contraception or any other commodity that has been advertised! It was solely the influence of the advert on the face of the ticket and in particular the presence of the logo and slogan, which to my mind effectively made it a new type. The presence of an advert on the back would often influence the layout and style of the front of the ticket anyway, particularly in those cases where Britannia was not the supplier of the company's ordinary ("definitive") rolls. Even when the title style was carefully copied, minor changes in font and spacing were likely to occur, again making a new type. Subsequently, no doubt through the advertising business, Britannia did win contracts for the production of many ordinary non-advert rolls, as it does to this day. Examples are the standard rolls of Arriva, First and Stagecoach, along with those of smaller companies like Reading Buses and Solent Blue Line. Furthermore my own interest in the subject led to my taking over the editorial responsibility in Journal for advertising rolls from January 1998. However, I digress…

The next development occurred in late 2000, when the practice of including the logo on the front ceased altogether. From then on, up to the present day, there has been no reference to the advertiser on the face of the ticket. This change took place not long after both Kentucky Fried Chicken and Burger King revamped their logos and there is just one KFC example, on Reading Buses, and five BK examples, one on East Yorkshire the others on First *f* York, Indeed, the very last ticket roll to sport an advertiser's logo was this First *f* York BK promotion valid to 15.10.2000 **(52)**.

(52)

This was the first feature introduced by Britannia - the advertiser's logo and a slogan on the face of some tickets. The other noteworthy feature was the inclusion of the bus operator's name on the **back** of the ticket, once again with a "Make the most of …" style slogan. This, too, was selective and only appeared with certain promotions - here seen with McDonald's (Sovereign), KFC (East Kent) and Pizza Hut (Bee Line) **(53)**.

(53)

Initially there was a rather complex situation with some Pizza Hut and McDonald's adverts on Trent Buses and Barton rolls. These bore the names of both bus companies on the face, but were "personalised" to either Trent Buses or Barton on the back **(54)**. In addition there were rolls with just Trent Buses and just Barton titles on the front.

(54)

This was another feature that died out fairly quickly, and after 1995 it was generally only to be found with some Pizza Hut and Pizzaland adverts on Wayfarer tickets. It did survive for longer on Almex A90 tickets, such as those for Crosville, PMT and, especially, [Lincolnshire] Road Car & City Transport tickets which continued to carry the slogan right up until 2006, when the change to Stagecoach took place and the venerable Road Car title disappeared **(55)**.

(55)

At the time when Image Colour Rolls got going in 1993, several older types of ticket equipment were still in use and advertising rolls were produced for these machines. As already noted, the space available was generally much less than on a Wayfarer 2 or 3 ticket, so everything was much more condensed, but the same principles of multi-colour design were applied.

So we have examples of advertising rolls for:

Setright Speed   Cambus (KFC) - note use of white roll instead of the usual buff or blue; only known with Cambus, Eastern Counties and Viscount/Stagecoach Viscount.

Almex A   Maidstone & District (KFC) - note the M&D title on both front and back, plus the "Make the most of …" slogan **(56*)**.

(56*)

Almex Magnet   Stratford Blue (Pizzaland) - this one was titled on both front and back plus slogan; cf also the Go Ahead Gateshead tickets with BK logo on front (unique) **(47)**.

Timtronic   Oxford Bus Company (McD) - also titled on both sides plus slogan; only known with Oxford and Stagecoach Devon **(57*)**.

(57*)

Datafare   Milton Keynes Citybus/Buckinghamshire Roadcar (KFC) - title on back only plus slogan; Datafare adrolls are only known with those companies that came to form MK Metro Ltd.

Farestram   Southampton Citybus (Pizza Hut) - titled on both sides plus slogan. Only known with Nottingham City Transport, Preston Bus and Southampton Citybus **(58*)**; latter also with KFC logo on front (unique) **(47)**.

(58*)

* actual size

I mentioned earlier that the presence of an advert on the back would often influence the layout and style of the front of the ticket, thereby enhancing its interest. This is particularly evident with certain bus companies, whose advertising tickets were quite distinct from their definitive (non-advertising) rolls. Let us look at a few examples.

Sovereign Bus & Coach **(59)** had multi-coloured advert rolls right up to the time when they were taken over by Arriva (in 2004/05). In fact there was a progression through four distinct types, all of which are far more colourful than their definitive rolls, which were plain blue on primrose.

- 1st type includes Jetlink in green, and Welwyn & Hatfield Line (1994-96).
- 2nd type GreenLine added, with Jetlink now in yellow (1997-98).
- 3rd type Jetlink disappears following restructuring of National Express and "Shuttle" added below GreenLine, in red (1999-2000).
- 4th type Welwyn & Hatfield Line disappears and GreenLine loses its "Shuttle" epithet (2001-03). But note the continued use of red, just for the dot in GreenLine!

(59)

Plymouth Citybus **(60)**, by contrast, had black rolls in a quite different design to the red definitives. These went through three different types, all in the same general style, with variations to the spacing and number of lines below "Citybus" (one or two).

(60)

Maidstone & District **(61)** had two successive title styles for advertising tickets, both quite different from the definitive. The first one was the same as that used on their Almex A tickets (3 promotions in 1996). The second employed the scroll logo, evocative of the company's pre-NBC days (3 promotions in 1997).

(61)

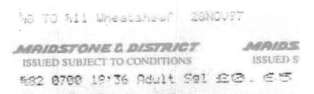 

Sister companies Teesside Motor Services, Tees & District and United Automobile Services also had black advert rolls. These were quite different from the definitives, which were printed in yellow/brown on white roll (TMS), red on yellow roll (Tees) and red on white roll (United). Advert rolls always had joint TMS and Tees titles.

- 1st TMS & Tees type with a Middlesbrough telephone number (1993-97).   )
- 2nd TMS & Tees type with an 0345 telephone number (1997).   ) **(62).**

All the TMS & Tees rolls carried the advertisers logo and slogan on the front.

(62)

- 1st United type with Darlington telephone number (1993-97)   )
- 2st United type with an 0345 telephone number (1998)   ) **(63).**

(63)

All except for two United rolls carried the advertiser's logo and slogan on the front (63A).

(63A)

These companies became part of Arriva in 1998, but for a year or so the Arriva advert rolls were of a unique style (64), including a "serving the North East" identifier and the 0345 telephone number (two rolls known). In 2000 this changed again to the Traveline number (only one roll known), but after that standard Arriva fronts were the order of the day.

(64)

 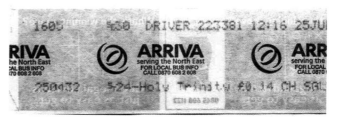

London & Country advert rolls were black with a red ampersand, contrasting with all-green definitives, except for one roll (a national KFC promotion), which had an all-black title, presumably by mistake (65).

(65)

Thamesway of Basildon was another company that had an interesting range of ticket fronts for promotional rolls, especially in the years following purchase by First Group in 1996. These changed almost as frequently as new promotions appeared and reflected some nuances that never found their way on to the definitive rolls, which were of course supplied in much greater quantities and lasted longer in service.

Compare these tickets with the original definitive:

- 1st type with logo featuring Tower Bridge and a Thames sailing barge either side of the River Thames + Basildon helpline number 287541 (1995 - 2 promotions).
- 2nd type similar but with helpline number changed to 525251 (1995-96 - 3 promotions) (66).

(66)

- 3rd type now with a prominent *f* logo, still with the same helpline number (1997-98 - 3 promotions) **(67).**

(67)

- 4th type shows the title as First *f* Thamesway and we can note conversion from Wayfarer Mk 2 to Mk 3 (1998 - just one promotion).
- 5th type the telephone number changes to Chelmsford and is now referred to as Customer Services (1998-99 - 3 promotions) **(68).**

(68)

- 6th type the telephone number changes again to 0345 and is Essex Traveline (1999 - 1 promotion).
- 7th type 0345 changes to 08457 and is rebranded Essex County Council Traveline (1999-2000 - 2 promotions, including one by First Great Eastern for its Summer Saver Card).
- 8th type sees the appearance of both the National Traveline and Thamesway's own Customer Services numbers (2001 - 1 promotion) **(69).**

So there were 16 promotions with 8 different fronts! After that, tickets carried the titles of First *f* Eastern National, First *f* Thamesway and First *f* Airport Bus & Coach. Sister Essex Buses company Eastern National also went through an interesting progression of fronts, reflecting several of the styles we have seen with Thamesway.

(69)

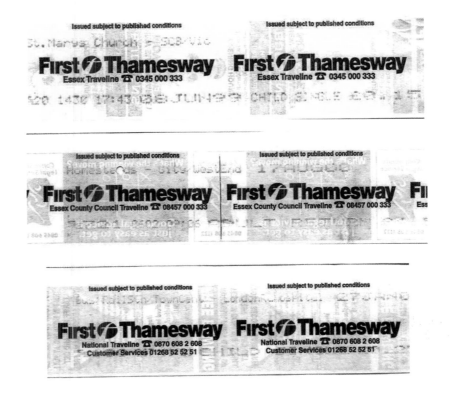

Midland Fox had definitive tickets printed in red on yellow roll. There was a progression of advert tickets:

- 1st type in red on white roll, with outline drawings of single and double deck buses interspersed - The Midland Fox Group (1993).
- 2nd type similarly with the buses coloured-in yellow (1993-94).
- 3rd type "Group" was dropped (1994-96) **(70).**

(70)

- 4th type was of a new design, similar to the new definitive but with conditions over the logo and title instead of interspersed (1996-98) **(71).**

(71)

This is an appropriate point to mention that Keith Edmondson continued to produce advertising tickets, although in far smaller quantities. Keith did one roll for Midland Fox (Zûû Club, Hinckley) and this is modelled on the later (blue) definitive, but is quite distinct from those produced by Britannia **(72).**

(72)

Amongst Keith's other products, we can also note promotional rolls for:

- Aylesbury & the Vale - one of the original operating divisions of The Shires [others included Chiltern Rover, Watford & District], but not otherwise used on tickets (John Menzies).
- Orion, Wemyss Bay (various advertisers in the Greenock area).
- Harte Buses, Greenock (more advertisers in the Greenock area).
- Handy Bus, Warminster (Halifax Property Services) **(73).**

(73)

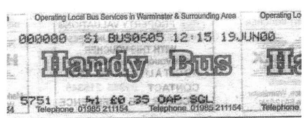

Others include:

- Leicester Citybus in 1995 (with which, I understand, he encountered considerable difficulty satisfying his client, Woolworths).
- Northern Bus (BK).
- Redby Bus & Coach, Sunderland (BK plus several self-adverts).
- Stagecoach Perthshire - another oddball title for what is now Stagecoach in Perth (John Menzies).
- Blue Bus Services, Derby (a whole string of Berlins Bar promotions).
- First Stop Travel, Renfrew (2004 and possibly the last advert roll done by Keith).

There were several more, including some which were untitled, eg: Felix Bus Services, Stevensons and Yorkshire Terrier.

Keith's philosophy these days is that the whole process tends to constitute too much hassle to generate much profit, with both the advertiser and the bus company having to approve the finished product and sometimes with uncertain prospects of getting paid...

Another player in the field for a relatively short time in 1999 was a firm of paper converters called Tayrol Ltd. of York, who produced a whole series of rolls for First York featuring local advertisers **(74)**. The fronts were all identical, but the backs contained 7 advert panels, arranged vertically. One of these panels read "To advertise here" with a contact name and number. The first batch of rolls, first noted in September 1999, had Lee or Derek as the contact names, whist the second batch, out by November 1999, had just Lee. Of the first batch I believe there are at least twenty one rolls with different combinations of advertisers - most appearing on more than one roll - and I still have several oddments which don't fit into any of the known combinations, so there are probably more. The situation was further compounded when the second batch came out, with many new advertisers but including some of the original ones. Of the second batch I have identified twelve rolls with different combinations, but I still have a further fifteen oddments that cannot be matched, so there are probably many more. I have counted no fewer than seventy five advertisers plus a few unidentified snippets indicating at least three more! The whole thing was a short-lived phenomenon, but presumably made no money for Tayrol, as it ceased in early 2000 and there has been no evidence of any similar activity since†. But then, who knows what might have taken place between Britannia and Tayrol (pure speculation on my part)?

---

†   *This has subsequently proved incorrect, as Tayrol produced a further promotional roll for First York (see May 2008 Journal page 190). Ticketmedia has since disavowed any knowledge of Tayrol.*

(74)

When First Group and Stagecoach changed from naming individual companies to their now ubiquitous titles, a number of short-lived "transitional" types appeared only on advert rolls (except for First Mainline - see below).

Let's look first at First, who rationalised their image and introduced the "transforming travel" strapline in 2001. By the end of that year the change was underway and local identities began to disappear:

- Beeline - the transitional version (2 promotions) is very similar in layout to the new standard design, but is printed entirely in black **(75).**

(75)

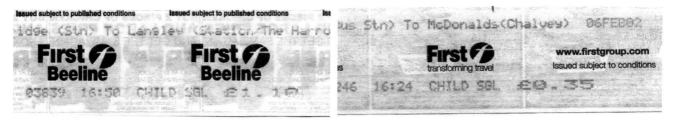

- Bradford - another company with a succession of different designs and colours. There are two transitional versions, one coloured pink (2 promotions), the other green (one promotion); note the change in the website address. This then changed to corporate (blue and magenta) colours without the "thank you" message **(76)**. Remarkably, Bradford advert rolls still appear in this design, complete with local telephone number! How do they get away with it? The only minor change is that the text at the foot now omits the word "published".

(76)

- Leeds - here the pink transitional tickets simply omitted reference to Leeds (2 promotions) **(77)**. These two tickets were issued on the same bus on the same day - a lucky find!

(77)

- Leicester's rather plain, red rolls became even plainer (2 promotions) **(78)**.

(78)

- Mainline - once again, the transitional rolls simply omitted reference to Mainline (one promotion) **(79)**. However it just so happened at this time that Mainline ran its own offer in connection with launch of the "Overground" network of routes. On the definitive rolls, also in transitional style, further details of the offer were set out on the back, but there were also two promotional rolls that carried the offer text on the front **(79A)**. The ringed number indicates an Overground route and there were five different rolls (for both promotions), all showing a combination of four route numbers. It's all explained in more detail by Dave Aspinwall in January 2002 *Journal* (page 13).

(79)

(79A)

- Manchester - by now using ERG Prodata equipment. First Manchester (which consistently appeared without the "*f*" logo, probably as an error that just got repeated) changed to First *f* (3 promotions). By 1 December 2001 the machines had been reprogrammed to print just First *f*, so there were further variations to be found **(80)**.

(80)

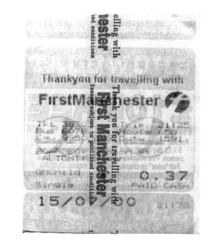

- Midland Red [West] - still on Wayfarer 2 at the time. Like Beeline, the transitional rolls were similar in layout to the new standard design, but printed entirely in red like their predecessors (2 promotions) **(81)**.

(81)

- Western National (Almex A90). The title appears in blue on the back and the front is blank, like earlier First *f* Western National issues (2 promotions) **(82)**.

(82)

No transitional advert rolls are known for any of the other First Group companies.

More recent variations - First Essex Buses rolls with driver recruitment text on front (this used to appear on the back of definitive rolls), mostly with Colchester telephone number, as here, but examples are known with Basildon and Chelmsford numbers **(83)**.

(83)

Now let's have a look at Stagecoach, whose move towards standardisation started a little earlier, in mid-2000. Here the change was to red-printed rolls titled Stagecoach Holdings plc. The transitional advertising rolls had "Holdings plc" in lower case text within a solid line below the Stagecoach title. This soon changed to upper case text within three underlines and this remained the interim standard until the current blue "bouncing ball" logo style was introduced in January 2001. There are only a few transitional issues known, each lasting for one promotion only, indicating that the change took place fairly quickly:

- Coastline Buses **(84)**.

(84)

- Hampshire Bus **(85)** - note inclusion of the clip marks along the top edge, carried over from the previous design. An example of the interim standard Stagecoach Holdings plc Wayfarer 3 roll is also shown (Hampshire Bus).

(85)

- Hartlepool **(86)** - identical layout to the Coastline version. The blue version with the full title is also quite scarce, having only been known on two promotions in 1997.

(86)

- Several ERG Prodata issues, eg: East Midland, Manchester **(87)** and maybe others. There is a "Stagecoach" watermark along the edges, not very visible.

(87)

Although definitive ERG rolls appeared for a short time with the title "Stagecoach the integrated transport company", no such advertising rolls are known.

When Arriva burst upon us in spring 1998, there were no transitional types. The old British Bus group titles gave way to the new standard Arriva rolls and it has been that way ever since. However we have already noted the existence, for a short period of time, of rolls titled "Arriva serving the North East" **(64)**. There was another example of "local initiative" applied to Arriva advertising ticket fronts and this was with Arriva The Shires **(88)**. In fact there were two distinct types, the first "serving the Shires", in use from 1998 to 2000 (19 promotions known), the second "serving the Shires & Essex", from 2000 to 2001 (10 promotions). The second roll reflected changes in the management structure, whereby the East Herts & Essex (former Townlink) operations were grouped with the Shires and managed from Luton. As with the North East, these titles only appeared on advertising rolls and eventually succumbed to the standard design.

(88)

Advertising promotions also brought some titled rolls to operators who otherwise used only plain tickets. Britannia has the admirable policy of printing the operator's title on rolls they produce (but not necessarily where this is applied by the machine itself, as with certain Almex A90, ERG Prodata and Wayfarer TGX150 users). The massive "Community Legal Service" government promotion in 2000 included some such operators, along with others from time to time, and so titled tickets appeared **(89)** for:

- North Rider of Newcastle-upon-Tyne - unusually with the advert on the face of the ticket (and a blank back).
- Pathfinder of Newark, which got absorbed into Nottingham City Transport (Wayfarer 3).
- Sheffield Omnibus, before amalgamation with Andrews.
- Silver Star of Caernarfon.
- TJ Walsh of Halifax.

(89)

Ads on Tix (A Review of Commercial Advertising on UK Transport Tickets)

- First *f* Pennine of Dukinfield, before being absorbed into First Manchester (both Almex A90 and ERG Prodata).
- Pathfinder of Newark - again (Almex A90).
- Richards Bros of Cardigan (Almex A90) - now have titled Wayfarer 3 tickets.
- Safeguard Coaches of Guildford (Almex A90) **(90).**

(90)

In addition, advertising rolls have produced titles and styles that have not otherwise appeared on the definitive versions, just as we saw with Thamesway, Plymouth Citybus and Midland Fox. These include:

- A1 Service (Ayrshire Bus Owners) - in 1994 plain rolls were normally used, but subsequent titled definitives were of a completely different style.
- Derby City Transport - the only ticket to bear both Blue Bus and City Rider titles, on a Derby Evening Telegraph advert of July 1996.
- Cambus - experimented with Wayfarer 3s in 1994 at Ely depot and 2 promotional rolls were produced. The title is unique since by the time the company eventually converted from Setright to Wayfarer, it was part of Stagecoach.
- First *f* Northampton - contemporary definitives had jointly titled rolls with First Leicester, then "First Group" titled rolls **(91).**

(91)

- Lowland *f* and SMT *f* - the only known use of rolls with the "*f*" logo before Lowland and SMT became part of First Edinburgh. **(92)**

- Stagecoach Fife - instead of Stagecoach Fife Buses. One promotion only, in 1999.

(92)

- Liverline, then North Western Liverline and Wigan Bus - all used North Western definitives or blank rolls prior to becoming part of Arriva in 1998. The North Western promotional rolls were similar, but not identical, to the definitive **(93)**.

(93)

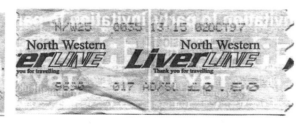

- Almex Magnet tickets of Stagecoach Cheltenham District, Gloucester Citybus, Swindon & District and Stroud Valleys **(94)** - definitives were not specific to the individual operator, just titled "Stagecoach". There was quite a complex progression of styles from NBC days through the early Stagecoach era, which would probably merit a topic of its own. In addition, Wayfarer 3 tickets for Gloucester Citybus (only) **(94A)** were produced in 1998-2000.

(94)

(94A)

- More Magnets - Provincial *f* and First *f* Provincial **(95)** - prior to conversion to Wayfarer 3. Unfortunately I have been able to find no issued example of the sole Provincial *f* promotion - for Littlewoods in 1997, although three different rolls were produced. And don't ask why a 1p excess fare should be charged!

(95)

- Town & Country Buses of Grays, which then became Town & Country Travel of Purfleet, whose subsequent titled rolls were in a quite different style. The firm is now defunct. The "Buses" ticket is from an unknown printer, whereas "Travel" is definitely a Ticketmedia product.

- And finally a red-printed ticket from Stagecoach Grimsby Cleethorpes - all the other promotional issues were yellow (or orange) **(96)**.

(96)

Perhaps we should mention here the numerous Wayfarer rolls that have been produced over the years for Solent Blue Line. This really is a topic in its own right since the variety is so great, and is not confined to advertising rolls. Here we are talking not about advertiser's logos, but many differing designs featuring Solent Blue Line's own services and facilities, complete with slogans, pictograms and natty line drawings. Most of these features also appeared on their definitive rolls, but often in a different sequence. Latterly there would be four different rolls produced for a single advertising promotion, each with a different mixture of frontal designs. It could be quite challenging to get them all and I have made many visits to Southampton and Eastleigh for this purpose over the last ten years. Solent Blue Line was one of the few bus companies to commemorate the Queen's golden jubilee on its tickets in 2002, and the golden jubilee motif appeared on both plain and advert rolls **(97)**.

(97)

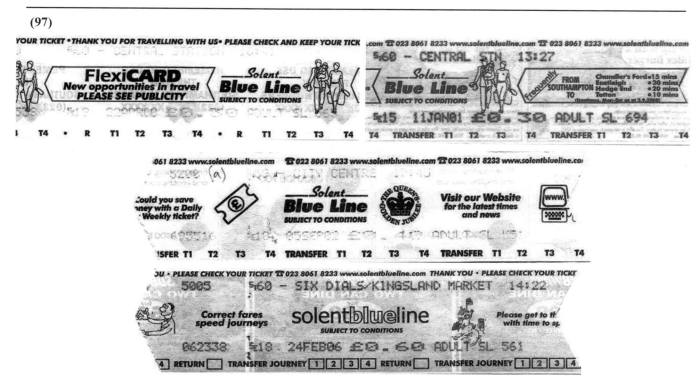

The scope of products and services being advertised has shown a steady change over the years. In 1993/94 it was almost wall-to-wall fast food, with just the occasional entertainment or leisure activity such as Riva Bingo or Super-Bowl 2000. The dominant advertisers were McDonald's, Kentucky Fried Chicken, Burger King and Pizza Hut. In 1995 Littlewoods joined the fray, mostly advertising their restaurants. By then also, numerous adverts were appearing for nightclubs, often linked with alcoholic drinks offers - Discotheque Royale, Volts, Utopia, Kiss, Zeus, Berlins, Xanadu, Lexington Avenue, Pure, Cairos … and many others. This subsequently ceased and no alcoholic beverage is now promoted as a matter of policy.

Other retail outlets began to appear, such as Aldi, Asda, Budgens, TJ Hughes, Index Catalogue Shops, TK Maxx, Three Cooks Bakery - but these have always been in the minority. More fast food outlets signed up, like Uncle Sams along the south coast, various pizza chains and Subway, who have run numerous campaigns over the past 10 years. Then we saw the government sector using the medium of bus tickets to advertise services to the community, both at national and local levels. Typical examples are community legal services, NHS Direct, gum - don't drop it, bin it, various adult education initiatives, benefits such as New Deal for Lone Parents, tax & benefits advice lines.

More recently there has been a proliferation of local government and community advertising of helplines for domestic violence and abuse, contraception and various support services for stopping smoking, drug awareness and the like. The adult education sector also advertises its courses, particularly around the beginning of the academic year. We have also seen adverts for the armed services, National Rail (Central Trains and First GE), National Express (on others operator's tickets) and Stena line. BT has been a long-running advertiser with its "Free return" campaigns, but not recently. Add a smattering of cinemas, theatres, bingo establishments, casino slots, staff recruitment, photographic services, police anti-crime, washing powder and mobile telephone ringtones and you get a cross-section of late 20th / early 21st century society. There have even been attempts to woo the motorist, with advertising by the AA, Avis car hire and Easy rent-a-car. The variety is endless and will no doubt continue to grow. However, few of these advertisers had any influence over the frontal design of bus tickets and so, to me, are of secondary interest. Illustrated is a selection of non-fast food adverts (all Almex A90) giving a flavour of the variety:

- Snappy Snaps - Brighton & Hove.
- Boots the Chemist - Nottingham City Transport.
- East Lindsey Council - Road Car.
- NHS Direct (bilingual) - Richards Bros. (titled on front only)
- BT - Trent and Barton.
- Royal Navy and Marines - Western National **(98).**

(98)

No survey of advertising tickets would be complete without reference to some of the special bus ticket rolls produced by Ticketmedia. These did not affect the fronts of the tickets, but were unusual in other ways. The following are known:

- Scented rolls. These were first produced in connection with a Radion (washing powder) promotion in 1997 - the tickets were impregnated with a pungent niff. Others include Bewley's coffee, American Pie (the film, but with an apple smell!), Twix, Fanta and Lemon KitKat **(99).**

(99)

- Tactile tickets **(100)**. Firstly, heat sensitive tickets - the second Radion promotion, this time with a "disappearing stain", which duly returns a few moments later! In 2006 a York Dungeons advert on First York tickets carried a heat-sensitive panel revealing a new dungeon feature called "Labyrinth of the Lost".

(100)

- Secondly, scratch-off rolls. Nintendo Magazine - only with London Transport Buses and First Thamesway over the Christmas 1998 period **(100A)**. A familiar technology: scratch away a panel treated with abrasive ink, this time to reveal either the Nintendo logo or a "sorry, try again" panel. These panels were intermixed on the ticket rolls. If you got the logo, you could send the ticket off and enter a prize draw.

(100A)

- There were two other novelties over the same period, just with London Transport Buses. One featured a 3-D roll for Lego Znap **(101)** . This was supplied for use on certain Routemaster-operated services, complete with a box of 3-D glasses carried by the conductor! I remember giving the glasses out to several slightly bemused passengers on a number 8 bus in December 1998!

(101)

- The other was a metallic foil roll for Max Factor **(101A)**. This must have been very expensive to produce and is printed in black on a very shiny, slightly creamy-coloured paper foil roll (difficult to reproduce). Nothing like these last three rolls have appeared since that time, now over eight years ago, although they are still to be found featured on Ticketmedia's website.

(101A)

Let us make a brief digression into the wonderful world of art and look at a few of the more memorable tickets.

- South London Gallery, Peckham - LT Buses (June 2000 - six different rolls). These were the product of a public art project entitled route 12-36, London Central's two Routemaster-operated routes on which the tickets were issued. According to the Gallery's press release, the phrases were assembled from snippets of mobile phone conversations, shop, street and road signs, and fly-posters stuck on lamp posts along the bus routes. The tickets are fully documented in August 2000 *Journal* (page 292) **(102)**.

(102)

- Hamfisted! Children's and young people's art from thirteen schools plus Sutton Coldfield YMCA and the Mere Green Centre - Travel West Midlands (August 2003 - six different rolls). Real art in miniature **(102A)!**

(102A)

- Britart.com - LT Buses (October 2000). Wayfarer Clipper and Almex Microfare 3 versions. Note the different dimensions of the "artwork"! Microfares were used experimentally by conductors from Battersea garage on route 19. However the Clippers were eventually replaced by Cubic Handheld Ticketing Machines, capable of reading Oystercards, in May 2004 **(103).**

(103)

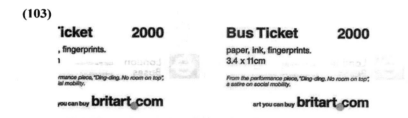

- Carlton TV Routes of Rock - LT Buses (August 1999 - at least three different rolls). An example of one medium (TV) advertising on another **(104).**
- Art at the Centre - Reading Buses TGX150 (Dec 2002 - four different rolls), but only on Daytrack/Nightrack services. This is one of the few promotions that has been mentioned in *Buses* magazine, whose correspondent thought so much of the designs that he urged readers to go to Reading and get a ticket. As is so often the case, by the time the magazine was out the rolls had been exhausted **(104A).**
- [insertspace] - Nottingham City Transport Almex A90 (April/May 2006). Another piece of bizarre creativity. Described in May 2006 *Journal* (page 176) **(104B).**

(104)   **(104A)**   **(104B)**

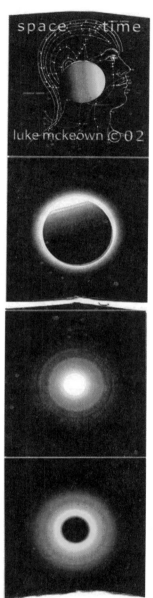

- Bulkhead Exhibition Venues - First Glasgow (August 1998). Not Ticketmedia, but AT&T Systemedia rolls, advertising an art exhibition on Glasgow buses, which ran from November 1997 to October 1998. The front of the ticket featured a most unusual design **(105).**

(105)

Just occasionally things go awry **(106)**!

- Colchester Borough Transport had a golf course promotion in 1995, but the tickets appeared with a McDonald's logo on the front.
- The Bee Line Buzz Company, in Manchester, was supplied with a McDonald's, Rochdale, advert roll in 1994 - but the front bore the title and logo of The Bee Line (ie: the Bracknell one)!

(106)

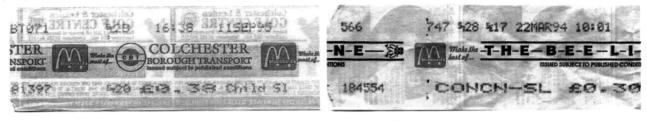

- Sometimes a colour is omitted or the colour registration is out of alignment.
- The wrong expiry date has been known (ie: the previous year), as happened with a Pizzaland promotion for Yellow Buses, Bournemouth, and occasionally non-existent dates like 31.09 appear.
- For five consecutive promotions the wrong telephone number appeared on the front of Kinchbus tickets (01509 81<u>65</u>37 instead of 01509 81<u>56</u>37). A simple transposition, but you got through to a fax machine instead of the Wellglade Group office! I drew this to the attention of Ticketmedia and in due course the error was corrected - so the Society has made a small contribution to the world of advertising tickets! Kinchbus themselves presumably didn't notice it.

To bring us completely up-to-date, let us take a brief look at a quite recent phenomenon - "security" tickets. These are not, of course, restricted to advertising rolls, but often the feature makes its debut on such a roll. The general idea is that the ticket is printed with watermark, which will make photocopied day and longer-period tickets more difficult to pass off as genuine. Such tickets can be examined with a UV "reader" which will reveal the presence of a watermark and authenticate the ticket (or otherwise). In some cases additional text is printed warning potential fraudsters of this feature. The following are known:

- First [South Yorkshire] (Wayfarer 3) - ellipses + warning message (similar tickets have appeared with other First Group companies).
- First [Glasgow] - small squares along upper and lower edges (Wayfarer 3) - no warning message.
- Stagecoach - now in regular use on most ticket types: Wayfarer 3, TGX150 (South Wales only) and ERG - ellipses + warning message **(107)**.

(107)

- Arriva [The Shires] (Wayfarer 3) - ellipses + "fraud proof ticket" message.
- Arriva [Cymru] (TGX150) - ellipses + "Security Ticket" statement.
- Cardiff bus / bws Caerdydd - ellipses (Wayfarer TGX150) + "Security Ticket" statement **(108).**

- Brighton & Hove, Burnley & Pendle and Lancashire United (Wayfarer TGX150) - watermarks but no warning message.

Well, I must apologise to rail ticket collectors that you have had to wait so long for any further reference to advertising in this mode. The fact of the matter is that there has been relatively little, compared to that on bus tickets. Also, the presence of an advert on the back of the ticket has had only a limited influence on the design of the front. It was not until the advent of electronic ticketing that advertising returned to rail tickets, after an absence of many years.

So far as I am aware, advertising never appeared on the backs of early, mechanised tickets such as Omniprinter, Flexiprinter, Multiprinter, NCR51 and INTIS.

London Underground

However, since giving this address at Southwick, Brian Boddy has come up with an LT weekly season ticket issued in 1970 with an advert for a record on the back **(109),** from a group called Shocking Blue - maybe known to Paul Smith? This could well be one of a series from Penny Farthing Records, but it's the first one I can recall seeing. So, thanks for that, Brian.

(109)

It was not until 1992 that modern advertising on rail tickets started, when London Regional Transport pioneered an advert on the back of its UTS tickets for Mercury Communications **(110)**. At the time, Brian Pask commented in *Journal* "the last time that Underground tickets carried commercial (rather than "in house") advertising was probably in 1915/16, when the backs of Metropolitan Railway edmondsons advertised State Express cigarettes and Wrights Coal Tar Soap" - as we have noted earlier. It appears that Brian too was unaware of the LT season advert. So after a gap of 76 years, advertising made a comeback on Underground tickets. This first advert was on the back of the early, yellow-fronted UTS tickets, and had the effect of compacting the LRT conditions of issue above the magnetic stripe. By the time the next advert appeared, UTS ticket rolls had changed to the now-familiar pink-fronted design.

Further UTS adverts followed intermittently, some for use at specified stations only. The fronts of the tickets were unaffected, although the text progressed through several types over time, but the way the conditions of issue were accommodated on the back varied from one advert to another. This practice continues to the present day, although we are not seeing many adverts on UTS tickets these days. Apart from the very first Mercury promotion, most UTS advertising tickets have been printed by "printer 5" (ie: the 4-digit reference number on the back is in the 5000 series). Some have appeared with appropriate coloured triangles, for issue outside the central area, but many have had no triangles even though they have been issued throughout the whole Underground network. There was also, in 2001, an advert on the back of a 7-day Travelcard, with two different versions of a competition draw. Since both these cards appeared with all four coloured triangles and none, there were technically ten different cards to collect. I managed a grand total of zero! The front, however, was unaffected.

(110)

National Rail

The first advertisement on the back of APTIS and SPORTIS tickets occurred in October 1998, with promotions for Marks & Spencer and Walkers Crisps/Doritos (**111**). Great Western Trains issued the former, Scotrail and Connex the latter. In both cases the adverts occupy the whole of the back of the ticket, with conditions of issue accommodated on the face in a rather compressed form. A further point of interest is that each promotion (but not necessarily each individual advert within it) carries a unique form number. For APTIS tickets these run from 4599/500 to 4599/567, then from 4599/601 to 4599/602, the last one appearing in 2004. Some adverts only occupied the area above the magnetic stripe, with conditions of issue appearing below it and, of course, plain orange bands on the front of the ticket. From 2004 onwards Ticketmedia used the backs of APTIS tickets to try to drum up more business, with slogans such as "Advertising on Track" and "The Poster in your pocket". There were two distinct varieties of these tickets, first with all text in black, then in a variety of colours. Yet despite all this, no further commercial advertisements are known on either APTIS or "new generation" tickets such as Cubic, Tribute and Fujitsu Star.

(111)

APTIS Travel Cards (**112**). A National Army Museum advert in 1997 had some advertising material on the front of the ticket as well as a panel on the reverse, along with conditions of issue. In 2002 an advert for the JVC / World Cup Final occupied the whole of the reverse, with conditions of issue moved to the front of the ticket, as reported in August 2002 *Journal* (page 303).

(112)

SPORTIS promotional tickets run from 3594/50 to 3594/74 (25 in all). For the most part, advertisements on SPORTIS have mirrored those on certain APTIS promotions, generally with similar artwork (**113**). There were also adverts on the back of SPORTIS tickets from:

- "FastTrain" (form no. 3594/HX) from the early days of Heathrow Express in 1998 - British Airways.
- Gatwick Express (form no. 3594/GA) - Easy Jet.

Was there also an advert for the Stansted Express?

(113)

Light Rail Systems

- Docklands Light Railway - Just two adverts have been reported - in August 2001 *Journal* (page 296) and August 2002 *Journal* (page 303). These occupy the whole of the back of the ticket. The conditions of issue on the face are simply modified to read, "Issued subject to published conditions" instead of "Issued subject to conditions - see over".

- Croydon Tramlink (one only known, for Nescafe, from start-up in 2000).

- Manchester Metrolink (one only known, for McDonald's).

- South Yorkshire Supertram (from the days when ticket vending machines were in use; since then there have been numerous adverts on the conductor-issued Wayfarer Clipper tickets). **(114)**

(114)

- Glasgow Underground.

- Tyne & Wear Metro. I am not aware of any advertising on the larger format tickets issued at stations on the recent extension to South Hylton. **(115)**

(115)

Miscellaneous

We can just touch on adverts appearing on larger format card tickets - here are two examples, from Easylink, on Jersey, and the Scotguide Glasgow open-top tour bus **(116)**.

(116)

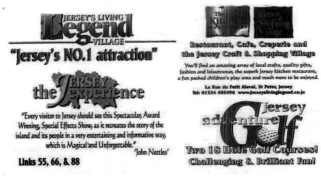

London Buses card passes for Embark Day, reported in November 1992 *Journal* (page 495) and April 1993 *Journal* (page 167), also featured a McDonald's advert on the reverse, and there were doubtless several others. An item that came to light after this address had been delivered is an advert for the Middleton Building Society on the front of some Saver Seven cards of the Greater Manchester PTE, in the early 1980s **(117)**. These cards had validity in the GMPTE area on both road and rail services and were validated through an Almex A machine in the issuing office.

(117)

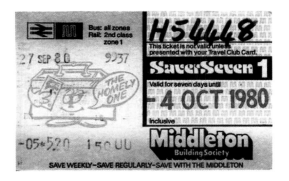

I am well aware that there are other types of ticket with commercial advertising, such as park-and-ride tickets dispensed from Metric Accent and other machines; tickets from minor railways and various other transport-related concerns.

Advertisements on tickets will continue to appear just as long as goods and services are offered for sale and there is a perceived market amongst transport users. This has, perhaps, never been truer than in today's materialistic society. As a 1950's LT poster once proclaimed "Getting and selling we lay waste our powers". On that note I will conclude.

Closing acknowledgements:

- to Peter Fickweiler (Southwick) / Paul Smith (Manchester) for loan of a data projector and operating the laptop computer.
- to Brian Boddy for placing the notices in Journal and facilitation of the Southwick event.
- to Michael Stewart for photocopies of numerous pre-grouping railway tickets, and for permission to reproduce illustrations of LMS pull-out insert card advert tickets from his "Catalogue of British Platform Tickets to 1948".
- to Brian Pask for copies of several edmondson tickets, and for use of material published in his "Ticket History" series of occasional papers.
- to Peter Nichols for information on UTS and DLR tickets.
- to Roger Atkinson for a copy of the illustrations accompanying Jack Purton's 1972 address and also loan of a Go-Ahead Gateshead Almex Magnet ticket.
- to Paul Smith for a quantity of TIM tickets.
- to Geoff Budd for his invaluable catalogues of Wayfarer and other machine-issued tickets, and also loan of a Southampton Citybus Farestram ticket.
- to Joe Casey for examples of the GMPTE Saver Seven cards.

My thanks to you all.

Hugh Fisher
TTS Membership No.784

Advertising Logos on bus tickets

Advertiser	Operator	Title	Logo
Almex Magnet			
Burger King			
	Go-Ahead Gateshead	R	RO
	Go-Ahead Gateshead	R	R
Farestram			
Kentucky Fried Chicken			
	Southampton Citybus	R	R
Wayfarer 2/3			
ASDA			
	Blackburn Transport	G	G
	Stagecoach Ribble	B	B
Beefeater			
	Mainline	R	R
Blockbuster Video			
	LRT Lothian	Br	Br
Bulkhead exhibition venues †			
	First f Glasgow	BPi	BPi
Burger King			
	Bluebird	B	RO
	Clydeside 2000	RYBkB	RO
	Colchester Borough Transport	R	R
	East Yorkshire	R	R
	Eastern National	G	G
	Fife Scottish	R	RO
	Fife Scottish	R	R
	First f Aberdeen	B	B
	First f Cymru	B	B
	First f Huddersfield	R	R
	First f York	R	R
	G M Buses North	Y	Y
	Go-Ahead Gateshead	R	R
	Grampian Transport	G	G
	Greater Glasgow f	R	R
	Greater Manchester f	Y	Y
	Greater Manchester f	R	R
	Inverness Traction	B	RO
	Inverness Traction	B	B
	KCB Network	M	M
	Kelvin f	R	R
	Kingfisher f	R	R
	LRT Lothian	Br	Br
	LRT Lothian	Pi	Pi
	Luton & District	R	RO
	Mainline	RBk	RO
	Mainline	R	R
	Midland Red North	R	RO
	Midland Red North	R	R
	Midland Red [North]	R	R
	Ribble Buses	R	R
	Ribble Buses	B	B
	Rider York	R	R
	Rider York f	R	R
	SMT	G	RO
	SWT	R	RO
	SWT	R	R
	Stagecoach Cumberland	R	RO
	Stagecoach Cumberland	R	R
	Stagecoach Ribble	B	B
	Stagecoach United Counties	B	B
	The Shires	R	R
	TMS & Tees	Bk	RO
	Trent Buses	R	R
	United	Bk	RO
	United	Bk	Bk
	United Counties	BRO	RY
	United Counties	BRO	RO
	West Midlands Travel	R	R
	West Riding Buses	G	G
	Western	Br	RO
	Western	Br	Br
	Yorkshire Rider	R	R

Advertiser	Operator	Title	Logo
Burger King (new logo)			
	East Yorkshire	R	R
	First f York	R	R
Champions Club			
	Grampian Transport	G	G
	SMT	G	G
Chesterfield College			
	Stagecoach East Midland	B	B
Discotheque Royale			
	GM Buses North	Y	Y
	GMS Buses	B	B
Elgringo's			
	Yellow Buses Bournemouth	B	B
Homestyle			
	Trent Buses	R	R
Index Catalogue Shop			
	Strathclyde's Buses	Y	Y
Jolly Roger			
	Bluebird	B	RB
Kentucky Fried Chicken			
	Andrews Sheffield Omnibus	B	B
	Barton Buses	R	R
	Bee Line Buzz Company	R	R
	Beeline	Bk	Bk
	Beeline f	Bk	Bk
	Blackburn Transport	G	G
	Blue Buses	B	B
	CalderLine	G	G
	CalderLine f	G	G
	Cambus	B	R
	Coastline	R	R
	Colchester Borough Transport	R	R
	East Midland	BRO	R
	Eastern National	G	G
	First Manchester	R	R
	GM Buses North	Y	Y
	GMS	Y	Y
	GMS Buses	B	B
	Greater Manchester f	R	R
	Halton Transport	R	R
	Hants & Surrey	Y	R
	Hants & Surrey	Y	Y
	Harrogate & District	R	R
	Kentish Bus	Br	R
	Kentish Bus	Br	Br
	KHCT	B	B
	Kingfisher f	R	R
	LRT Lothian	Br	Br
	Luton & District	R	R
	Mainline	RBk	R
	Mainline	R	R
	Midland Red North	R	R
	Midland Red [North]	R	R
	Reading Buses	BrG	R
	Reading Buses	G	G
	Reading Buses	R	R
	Ribble Buses	BRO	RB
	Rider York	R	R
	Sheffield Omnibus	B	B
	Southern National	G	R
	Stagecoach Coastline Buses	Y	Y
	Stagecoach East Kent	Y	R
	Stagecoach East Kent	Y	Y
	Stagecoach East Midland	B	B
	Stagecoach Grimsby Cleethorpes	Y	Y
	Stagecoach Hants & Surrey	O	O
	Stagecoach Hants & Surrey	Y	Y
	Stagecoach [KHCT]	B	B
	Stagecoach Ribble	B	B

Advertiser	Operator	Title colour	Logo colour
Kentucky Fried Chicken (cont'd)			
	Stagecoach		
	South Coast Buses	Y	R
	Stagecoach		
	South Coast Buses	Y	Y
	Stagecoach United Counties	B	B
	Strathclyde's Buses	O	O
	Strathclyde's Buses	Y	Y
	The Bee Line	Bk	R
	The Bee Line	Bk	Bk
	The Shires	R	R
	TMS & Tees	Bk	R
	TMS & Tees	Bk	Bk
	Trent Buses	R	R
	United	Bk	Bk
	United Counties	BRO	RB
	West Midlands Travel	R	R
	Yellow Buses Bournemouth	B	R
	Yellow Buses Bournemouth	B	B
	Yorkshire Rider	R	R
	Yorkshire Traction	R	R
Kentucky Fried Chicken (new logo)			
	Reading Buses	R	R
Littlewoods (logo style L1a)			
	Bee Line Buzz Company	R	R
	Fife Scottish	R	R
	GM Buses North	Y	Y
	Grampian Transport	G	G
	Inverness Traction	B	B
	Luton & District	R	R
	Mainline	R	R
	Midland Red North	R	R
	Reading Buses	G	G
	SWT	R	R
	Stagecoach Cumberland *	R	R
	Stagecoach East Midland	B	B
	Stagecoach [KHCT]	B	B
	Stagecoach United Counties	B	B
	Tayside Buses	B	B
	The Shires	R	R
	TMS & Tees	Bk	Bk
	Western	Br	Br
	Western	M	M
	Yorkshire Traction	R	R
Littlewoods (logo style L1b)			
	Bradford Traveller f	R	R
	First f Bradford	R	R
	Southport	M	M
Littlewoods (logo style L1c)			
	Clydeside 2000	R	R
Littlewoods (logo style L2)			
	East Yorkshire	R	R
	GM Buses North	Y	Y
	Greater Manchester f	R	R
Littlewoods (logo style L3)			
	Clydeside	R	R
	Fife Scottish	R	R
	First f Glasgow	R	R
	Grampian f	G	G
	Greater Glasgow f	R	R
	Halton Transport	R	R
	Harrogate & District	R	R
	LRT Lothian	Pi	Pi
	Mainline	R	R
	Midland Red North	R	R
	Midland Red [North]	R	R

Advertiser	Operator	Title colour	Logo colour
Littlewoods (logo style L3) (cont'd)			
	Mainline	R	R
	Midland Red North	R	R
	Midland Red [North]	R	R
	Reading Buses	G	G
	SWT	R	R
	Stagecoach Cumberland	R	R
	Stagecoach East Midland	B	B
	Stagecoach [KHCT]	B	B
	Stagecoach Ribble	B	B
	Stagecoach United Counties	B	B
	Stagecoach Western Scottish	B	B
	Strathclyde's Buses	Y	Y
	The Shires	R	R
	Trent Buses	R	R
	Yorkshire Traction	R	R
Liverpool Empire			
	GM Buses North	Y	Y
McDonald's			
	A1 Service	B	B
	Bluebird	B	B
	Cambus	B	RY
	Clydeside	R	R
	Colchester Borough Transport	R	R
	Eastern National	G	R
	Eastern National	G	G
	Fife Scottish	R	R
	First f Glasgow	R	R
	GM Buses North	O	O
	Grampian f	G	G
	Grampian Transport	G	G
	Greater Glasgow f	R	R
	Greater Glasgow fg	R	R
	Greater Manchester f	Y	Y
	Greater Manchester f	R	R
	Halton Transport	R	R
	KCB Network	M	M
	Kelvin f	R	R
	Kentish Bus	Br	R
	LRT Lothian	Br	Br
	LRT Lothian	Pi	Pi
	Luton & District	R	RY
	Luton & District	R	R
	Mainline	R	R
	Midland Red North	R	RY
	Midland Red North	R	R
	Midland Red [North]	R	R
	Red Bus [North Devon] **	R	R?
	SWT	R	R
	South Yorkshire		
	Road Transport	B	B
	Stagecoach Cumberland	R	R
	Stagecoach East Kent	Y	Y
	Stagecoach East Kent	O	O
	Stagecoach East Midland	B	B
	Stagecoach Hants & Surrey	O	O
	Stagecoach United Counties	B	B
	Stagecoach Western Buses	B	B
	Strathclyde's Buses	Y	Y
	The Bee Line [in error}	Bk	R
	The Shires	R	R
	TMS & Tees	Bk	RY
	Trent Buses	R	R
	Trent Buses / Barton	R	R
	United	Bk	RY
	United Counties	BRO	RY
	West Midlands Travel	R	RYBk
	West Midlands Travel	R	RY
	West Midlands Travel	R	R
	Western	Br	Br
	Yorkshire Buses	G	G

Appendix   Advertising Logos on bus tickets

Advertiser	Operator	Title colour	Logo colour
McDonald's (cont'd)			
	Yorkshire Buses	R	R
	Yorkshire Traction	R	R
Megabowl			
	Stagecoach Ribble	B	B
Palace			
	Stagecoach Ribble	B	B
Pepsi Max			
	KHCT	B	B
	Stagecoach East Midland	B	B
	Stagecoach Ribble	B	B
	Stagecoach United Counties	B	B
	Yellow Buses Bournemouth	B	B
Pizza Hut			
	Barton Buses	R	R
	Bee Line Buzz Company	R	RBk
	Bee Line Buzz Company	R	R
	GM Buses North	Y	Y
	Grampian Transport	G	G
	Harrogate & District	R	R
	KCB Network	M	M
	Keighley & District	Pi	Pi
	KHCT	B	RBk
	KHCT	B	B
	Mainline	RBk	RBk
	Ribble Buses	BRO	RBk
	SMT	G	RBk
	SMT	G	G
	SWT	R	RBk
	SWT	R	R
	Stagecoach Cumberland	R	R
	Stagecoach Ribble	B	B
	Stagecoach Western Scottish	M	M
	Tayside Buses	B	B
	Transit	G	G
	United	Bk	Bk
	United Counties	BRO	B
	Yorkshire Rider	R	RBk
Pizzaland			
	Mainline	R	R
	Midland Red North	R	R
	Rider York	R	R
	Stagecoach Ribble	B	B
	Stagecoach United Counties	B	B
	Yellow Buses Bournemouth	B	B
Pleasure Island			
	Mainline	R	R
Power Drome			
	KCB Network	M	M
Reliance			
	Reading Buses	R	R
Richeys Fitness Club			
	Strathclyde's Buses	Y	Y
Riva Clubs			
	GMS Buses	B	B
Royals Amusements			
	Fife Scottish	R	R
	United	Bk	Bk
Shoe Shed			
	Midland Red North	R	R

Advertiser	Operator	Title colour	Logo colour
Snappy Snaps			
	Luton & District	R	R
	The Shires	R	R
Stevenage Festival			
	Luton & District	R	R
Superbowl			
	GMS Buses	B	B
	The Shires	R	R
Super-Bowl 2000			
	Greater Manchester ƒ	Y	Y
	Mainline	R	R
	Midland Red North	R	R
	Midland Red [North]	R	R
	Stagecoach East Midland	B	B
	Stagecoach Ribble	B	B
	West Riding Buses	G	G
TJ Hughes			
	Halton Transport	R	R
	Midland Red North	R	R
Talking Pages			
	Strathclyde's Buses	Y	Y
Tennessee Fried Chicken			
	SWT	R	R
The Yeller			
	Mainline	R	R
Volts			
	GMS Buses	B	B
Wakefield Training & Enterprise Council			
	West Riding Buses	G	G
Woolworths			
	Stagecoach Hants & Surrey	Y	Y

Key to colour codes

B	Blue
Bk	Black
Br	Brown
G	Green
M	Maroon
O	Orange
Pi	Pink
R	Red
Y	Yellow

*   Stagecoach Cumberland - Littlewoods logo style 1a unconfirmed

**   Red Bus [North Devon] - unconfirmed report

†   Not Image / Ticketmedia product